Chipper's Journey

Written by Kinjatta Dobbins
Illustrated by Malena Stidham

In loving memory of my grandparents

Milderd "Mudder" McDonald and Ventie Smith

Kinjatta Dobbins is the author of Lou Lou Mae's Badge of Courage. Chipper's Journey to America is her second picture book. Kinjatta got the idea for Chipper's Journey to America after a conversation she had with a pet store clerk about betta fish. Kinjatta lives in San Antonio, with her husband and children.

Malena Stidham's bold colors in her art reflect her diversity and multicultural backgrounds. It is important to her to transmit through her art emotional reactions and feelings through images and color.

Although she was born and raised in Lima, Peru, Malena lived most of her life in Miami, Florida. She attended Miami-Dade College, where she received a degree in Arts and Design. She also studied under the tutelage of Master Artist Wylene del Pino. Malena is an accomplished large-scale muralist who has created more than a dozen murals in South Florida and in Texas schools and public libraries. Malena resides in San Antonio, Texas, where she has a studio and teaches fine art to children. Chipper's Journey to America is her first commissioned work as an illustrator.

Chipper was so scared that he jumped. When he landed, he could hardly believe he had gone so far.

Lub, dub, lub, dub

Still in a panic, Chipper continued swimming until he hopped right into a shallow pond. He wanted to make sure he got far away from the betta who bullied him out of his home.

But before long, his new pond started to shrink. The big plops of water weren't coming down from the sky as often as they used to.

Eventually, his underwater hideaway disappeared except for tiny cracks filled with water at the bottom of the pond.

"Aargh!"

If he kept his scales wet, he could still breathe. Chipper flopped around in the tiny cracks, but the air was drying his scales, and the sunshine was making him too hot.

So with all his might, Chipper jumped again, hoping for more water.

Chipper was tired. He was just about ready to give up...then he saw a stream of water in the distance. Chipper jumped as fast as he could.

Suddenly, a strange-looking object scooped him from the water and dropped him into yet another odd place.

Bloop!

Chipper tried to swim away, but he was trapped. When he was too exhausted to try anymore, he settled to the bottom.

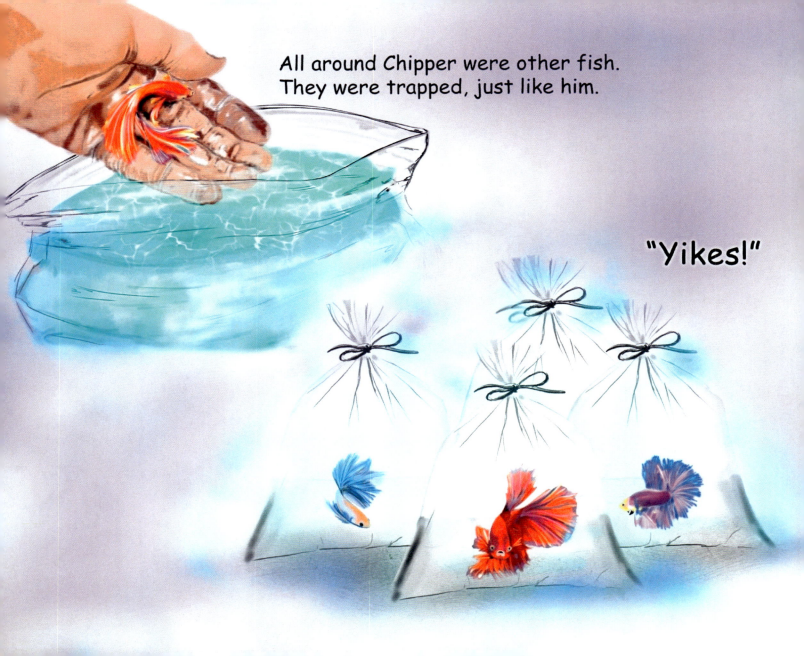

Chipper was dreaming of his old home when everything suddenly went black. He went on a long journey, wondering when he would get to see the light again.

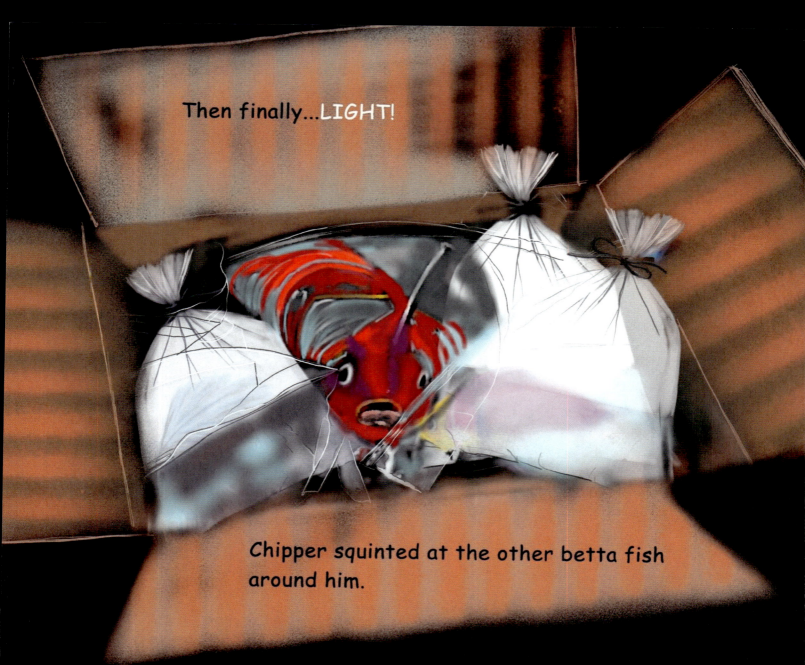

One by one, the other fish disappeared. When it was Chipper's turn, he felt the current pushing him toward the unknown.

Kerplunk!

Chipper was happy to finally have enough water to wiggle his fins. And to his surprise, funny-looking flakes were floating on the water. He swam up to smell them.

Chipper gobbled it all up then swam to the bottom doing his best to hide. He missed his old home, where he had plenty of privacy.

Big eyes followed Chipper's every move, but eventually, he learned to ignore them.

Then one day a boy picked up Chipper's container and looked at him very closely. Chipper saw kindness in the boy's eyes, so he cautiously swam toward them.

Lub dub, lub, dub

The boy beckoned excitedly for his mother to come and see Chipper. When the boy moved his finger around the sides of the container, Chipper followed.

The boy carefully brought Chipper's container down from the shelf. Holding it close to his chest, he whispered, "We're going home, fishy."

"Yay!"

Somehow, Chipper knew he was safe. The boy's gentle eyes made Chipper...happy. Instantly, Chipper was sure his new home would be perfect!

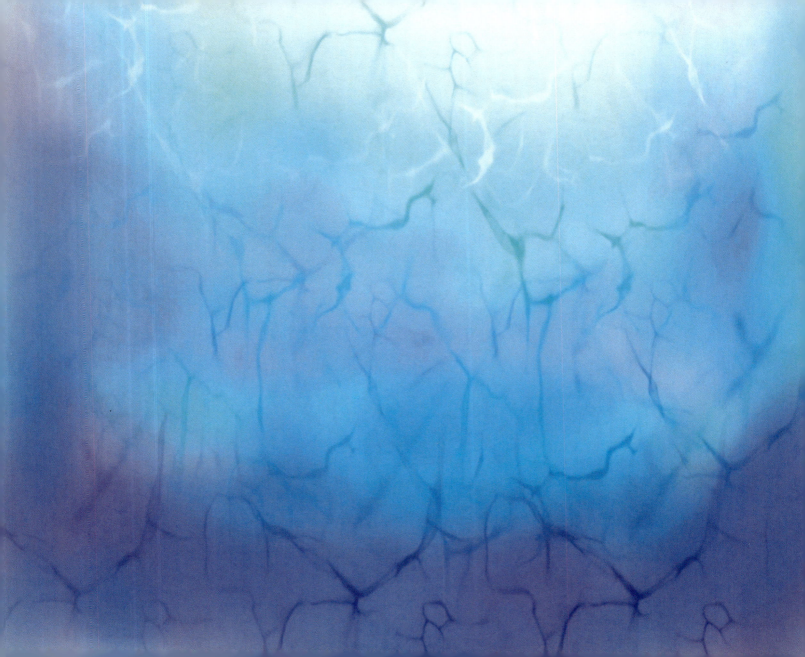

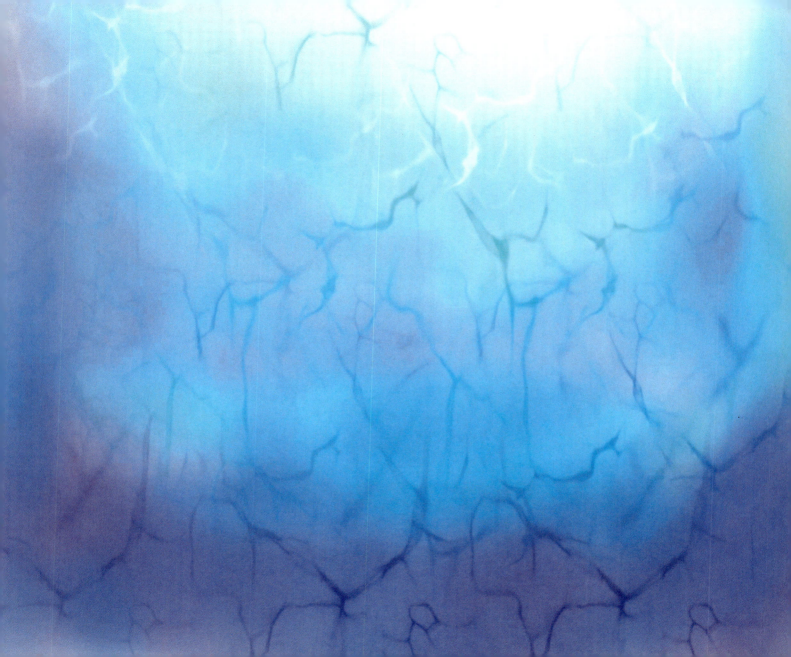

Made in the USA
Monee, IL
27 September 2021